Bennett Book

## DATAWORLD

# SPACE TALK

## ROBIN KERROD

**GRAFTON BOOKS**
A Division of the Collins Publishing Group

LONDON GLASGOW
TORONTO SYDNEY AUCKLAND

Grafton Books
*A Division of the Collins Publishing Group*
8 Grafton Street, London W1X 3LA

Published by Grafton Books 1986

*Copyright* © Lionheart Books 1986

*British Library Cataloguing in Publication Data*
Kerrod, Robin
　Space talk. — (Dataworld; V.3)
　1. Telecommunication systems — Juvenile literature
　I. Title　　II. Series
　621.38　　TK5102.4

ISBN 0-246-12712-0

This book was conceived, edited and produced by
Lionheart Books
10 Chelmsford Square
London NW10 3AR

*Editor* Lionel Bender
*Designer* Malcolm Smythe
*Picture Researcher* Dee Robinson
*Editorial Assistant* Madeleine Bender
*Illustrator* Rob Shone
*Typeset by* Dorchester Typesetting Group Ltd.

Printed and bound in Italy by
New Interlitho, Milan

All rights reserved. No part of this publication may be reproduced, stored in a retrieval system, or transmitted, in any form or by any means, electronic, mechanical, photocopying, recording or otherwise, without prior permission of the publishers.

# Contents

| | |
|---|---|
| Messages from Space | 8 |
| Satellites | 10 |
| Rocketing into Orbit | 12 |
| Shuttle Launch | 14 |
| Satellite Operations | 16 |
| Comsats | 18 |
| Earth Station | 20 |
| Live via Satellite | 22 |
| Special Networks | 24 |
| Weather Satellites | 26 |
| Landsats | 28 |
| Star Gazers | 30 |
| Probing the Planets | 32 |
| Views from Other Worlds | 34 |
| Radio Ears | 36 |
| Alien Messages | 38 |
| Milestones | 40 |
| Glossary | 41 |
| Index | 43 |

# Messages from Space

Tens of thousands of kilometres above the clouds, a family of tiny moons is speeding through space, keeping pace with the Earth as it spins round. In a blink of an eye, they relay, or pass on, voices, pictures, facts and figures from one country to another.

These tiny 'moons' are communications satellites, or comsats. They form part of a giant communications network that covers the world. Comsats handle the voices, pictures, and so on, in the form of coded radio signals. These are beamed up to them from the ground by giant dish-shaped aerials. The comsats then beam the signals back down to giant aerials in other countries.

Thanks to comsats we can instantly speak to people on the other side of the world, and on television see events that take place there as they happen. This kind of instant communication helps bring the peoples of the world closer together. It is creating what is sometimes called the 'global village', where everyone is a neighbour, no matter where they live.

**Space age information**
Communications is just one of the many fields that have been revolutionized by the Space Age. We are reminded of another when we see the television weather forecast. The forecasters show you pictures of the clouds taken by weather satellites. Farmers, foresters, surveyors, fishermen and mineral prospectors are among the people who use information provided by Earth-resources satellites such as Landsat, which constantly survey land and sea. Astronomers are making startling new discoveries from information beamed back to them from astronomy satellites and probes that venture deeper into space. One day, maybe tomorrow, they may receive the most important message of all – greetings from another civilization elsewhere in the universe.

One of the huge dish aerials at the Goonhilly earth station in Cornwall, England. It is used to beam signals up to, and receive them from, communications satellites that circle tens of thousands of kilometres above the Earth.

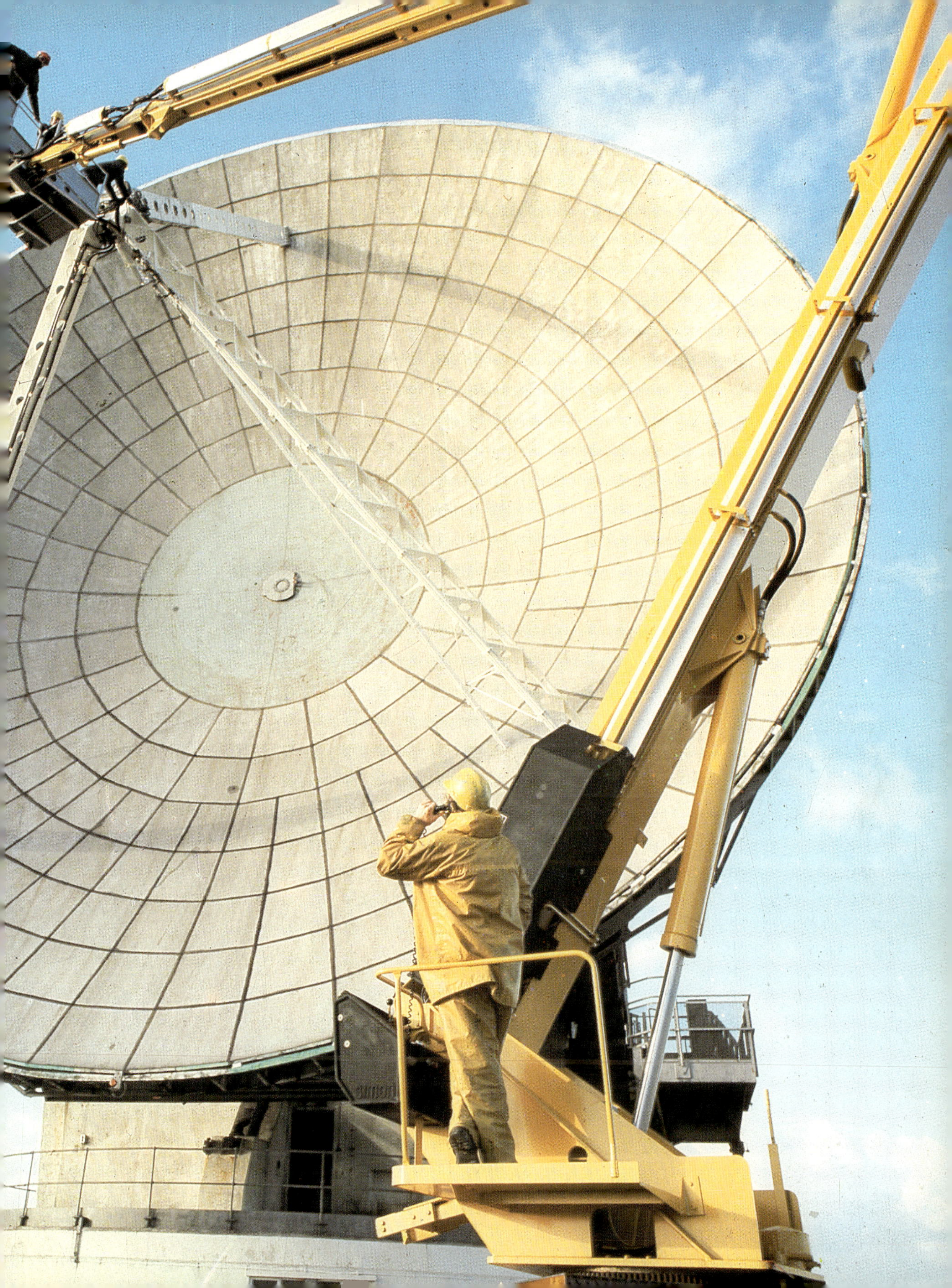

# Satellites

In ordinary life, we know 'what goes up, must come down'. This is because everything on Earth is held down by the powerful force of gravity. So how can we beat gravity and launch a satellite into space? The answer is by speed.

We shoot the satellite into the sky high above the atmosphere at the incredibly high speed of 28,000 kilometres an hour. And we guide it so that soon after lift-off it travels parallel with the ground. It then starts circling round and round the Earth in a path we call its orbit.

The satellite is actually falling towards the Earth. But the amount it falls due to gravity matches exactly the amount the Earth's surface curves. So in practice the satellite remains in orbit at the same height.

Another question you might ask is why doesn't the satellite slow down? The reason is that in space there is no air to slow anything down. So it just carries on travelling at the same speed.

If a projectile is fired from the Earth, it travels so far before being pulled back to Earth by gravity. The faster it is fired, the further it goes before falling back. If you could fire it at 28,000 km/h, it would go into orbit.

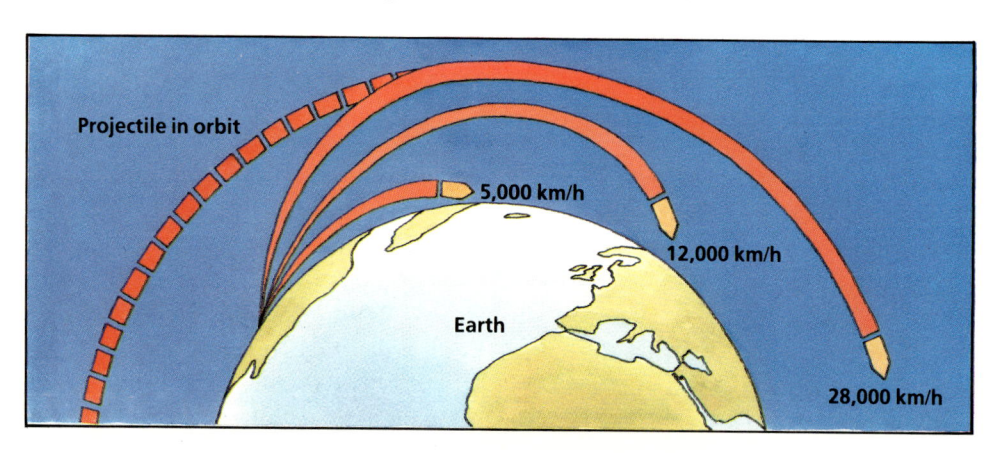

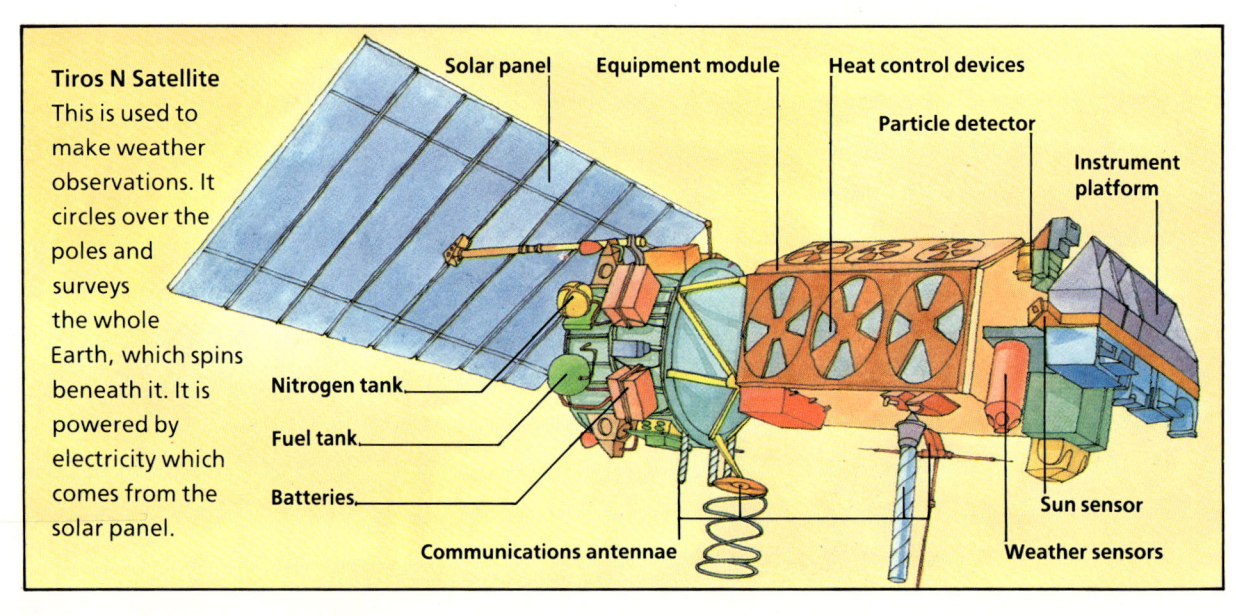

**Projectile in orbit**
5,000 km/h
12,000 km/h
Earth
28,000 km/h

**Tiros N Satellite**
This is used to make weather observations. It circles over the poles and surveys the whole Earth, which spins beneath it. It is powered by electricity which comes from the solar panel.

Solar panel — Equipment module — Heat control devices
Particle detector
Instrument platform
Nitrogen tank
Fuel tank
Batteries
Communications antennae
Sun sensor
Weather sensors

## Orbits high and low

Satellites can be launched into a variety of orbits round the Earth. Some orbits are nearly circular, others are very oval or egg-shaped. As you can imagine, the higher a satellite orbits, the longer it takes to travel round the Earth. At a height of about 300 kilometres a satellite takes just over 1½ hours to complete one orbit, and it makes about 15 orbits a day.

At a height of about 36,000 kilometres, a satellite takes just 24 hours to make one orbit. But this is the same time that it takes the Earth to spin round once. So if we place a satellite into such an orbit above the equator, it will appear to stand still in the sky. We call this orbit a geostationary orbit, or a Clarke orbit, after Arthur C. Clarke, the famous science-fiction author, who was the person that first suggested it. Most communications satellites are placed in geostationary orbit because it is much easier to beam signals to a satellite that is 'fixed' in the sky (see page 19).

The communications satellite ATS-6 undergoing tests at the Johnson Space Center at Houston, Texas. It was the sixth of the applications technology satellites (ATS) used by NASA to carry out communications experiments. Launched in 1974, it was used to beam TV programmes to Indian villages. It was huge. The umbrella-type aerial measured nearly 10 metres across. It operated until 1985.

### Satellite orbits

Satellites are launched into different kinds of orbit depending on their use. Many are put into orbit above the equator (1), others over the poles (2). A few are put into eccentric orbits (3); they travel close to the Earth at some times and far away at others.

# Rocketing into Orbit

To launch a satellite into orbit, we must give it a speed of 28,000 kilometres an hour. This is more than ten times the speed of the Concorde supersonic airliner!

The only kind of engine powerful enough to boost a satellite to such a high speed is the rocket. The rocket is also the only kind of engine that can work in space. Other engines, like Concorde's jet engines, have to 'breathe' air. They need the oxygen in the air to burn their fuel. In space there is no air, so these engines cannot work there. The rocket carries its own supply of oxygen to burn its fuel. Therefore it can work in space.

Two versions of the heavy launch vehicle Ariane, of the European Space Agency. Ariane 3 made its space debut in 1983. It is a three-stage rocket with two strap-on boosters which give it added thrust on take-off.

Ariane 4 is much bigger and is capable of launching heavier payloads into high orbit.

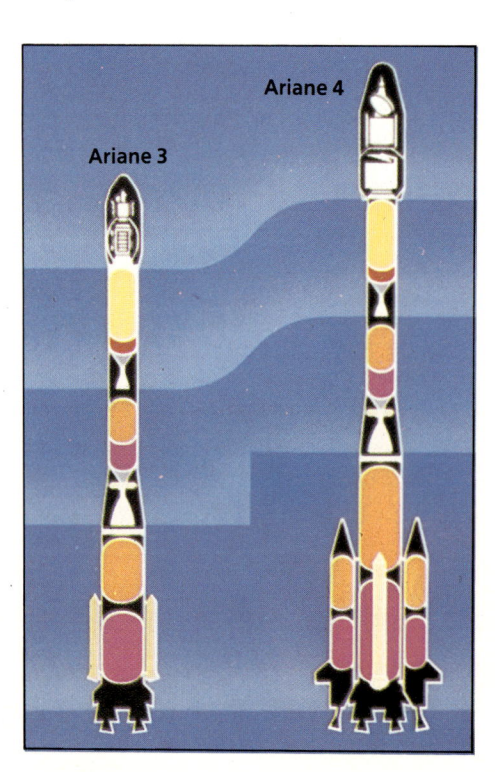

The main kind of rocket engine or motor used to launch satellites burns liquid fuels. A common fuel is kerosene, or paraffin. Another is liquid hydrogen. This is hydrogen gas cooled to such a low temperature ($-253°C$) that it becomes a liquid. The most common oxidizer, or substance rockets use to provide the oxygen, is liquid oxygen. This is oxygen gas cooled until it becomes liquid (at $-183°C$). The fuel and oxidizer are called propellants, because they push, or propel, the rocket forwards.

## Producing the thrust

In a liquid-fuel rocket motor, the propellants are pumped into a combustion chamber, where they mix and burn. The hot gases produced rush out of a nozzle at the rear of the rocket at high speed. As they shoot out backwards, they thrust the rocket forwards. This may seem strange, but it is similar to what happens when you blow up a balloon and let it go. As the air shoots backwards out of the neck, the balloon shoots forwards.

In practice, a string of rockets working one after another is needed to give a satellite the necessary speed to reach orbit. We call this arrangement a step-rocket or launch vehicle. Some launch vehicles use another kind of rocket to boost their speed at lift-off. It burns solid propellants. It is a more powerful version of a firework rocket.

Ariane blasts off the launch pad at the Guiana Launch Centre, near Kourou in French Guiana, South America. This is the main launch site for the European Space Agency.

Technicians installing a communications satellite into the nose cone of a Delta launching rocket at Cape Canaveral, in Florida USA, a few weeks before launching.

**Multi-stage Rocket**
A multi-stage rocket like Ariane takes off with the first stage and boosters firing together. The boosters fall away when their fuel has run out. The other stages are shed in turn, so the rocket becomes lighter and lighter as it travels faster and further.

13

Climbing on a pillar of smoke and flame, the space shuttle soars into the sky. In a little over 10 minutes, the orbiter Discovery will begin circling the Earth at a speed of 28,000 kilometres an hour.

The space shuttle stack (below) just about to leave the Vehicle Assembly Building, where it was put together.

# Shuttle Launch

Many satellites are now put into orbit by a very special kind of launch vehicle – the space shuttle. This is a manned vehicle that is part rocket, part spacecraft and part aeroplane. It takes off from the launch-pad like a rocket. In orbit it behaves like a spacecraft. When it returns from space, it lands on a runway like a plane.

Ordinary launch vehicles can be used only once. But the space shuttle can be used again and again. This makes space launchings much more economical. And the space shuttle can carry very much larger and heavier payloads (cargoes) than ordinary launch vehicles. It can carry objects up to 18 metres long and 4.5 metres across, which is nearly the size of a railway carriage!

## Shuttle design

There are three main parts to the shuttle system. The main one is the orbiter, which looks somewhat like an ordinary plane. The orbiter carries the payload and a crew of up to seven astronauts, both men and women. It is covered with some 30,000 tiles, which protect it when it returns through the atmosphere. At this time the friction (rubbing) of the air against the speeding orbiter produces tremendous heat. The tiles prevent this heat from harming the orbiter and the astronauts inside.

The orbiter rides piggy-back into space on a huge external tank, which carries fuel for the orbiter's three main rocket engines. Attached to the tank are two large booster rockets. All the rockets fire together to lift the shuttle off the launch pad. Then, first the boosters and afterwards the main tank separate from the orbiter as it climbs into orbit. The boosters parachute back to Earth and are recovered to be used again. The tank, however, is allowed to smash up in the sea. It is the only part of the shuttle system not to be used again.

There are four orbiters in the shuttle fleet – called Columbia, Challenger, Discovery and Atlantis. They are now shuttling into orbit up to ten times a year. They usually take off and land at the Kennedy Space Center in Florida, which has become the world's busiest spaceport.

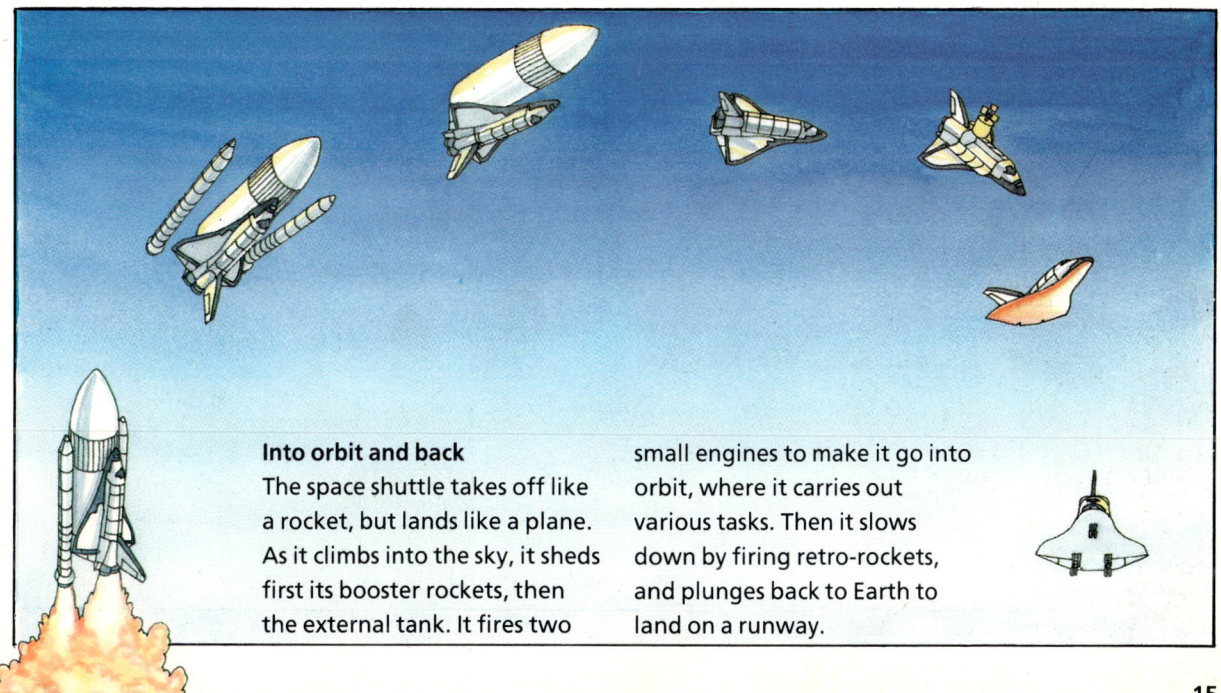

### Into orbit and back

The space shuttle takes off like a rocket, but lands like a plane. As it climbs into the sky, it sheds first its booster rockets, then the external tank. It fires two small engines to make it go into orbit, where it carries out various tasks. Then it slows down by firing retro-rockets, and plunges back to Earth to land on a runway.

# Satellite Operations

The shuttle orbiter carries satellites high above the Earth in its huge payload bay, which takes up most of the space in the craft. Several satellites are usually carried at the same time. Astronauts called mission specialists are responsible for launching the satellites from the bay. They work at a control panel at the rear of the orbiter's flight deck. They look out into the payload bay through windows.

Satellites may be launched from the bay in a number of ways. Some are literally sprung into space from pods in the bay. Some are spun sideways out of the bay rather like a frisbee. And others are lifted out by the orbiter's crane, a device called the remote manipulator system (RMS). The RMS is a long, jointed arm, with flexible joints and a 'hand' at the end that can grip objects. The RMS arm is used not only to place new satellites into orbit, but also to recover old, damaged or faulty satellites from orbit.

The shuttle is now used to recover and repair satellites that go wrong, such as Solar Max in April 1984.

## Recovery and repair

In 1984 the RMS arm was used in two spectacular recovery and repair missions. The stars of the missions were spacewalking astronauts, propelling themselves around in space with jet-powered backpacks called MMUs (manned manoeuvring units). In November 1984, astronauts Joe Allen and Dale Gardner, working from the orbiter *Discovery*, helped capture two 'dead' comsats. These satellites had gone into the wrong orbits nine months before. Discovery brought them back to Earth, where they were repaired and prepared for launching again.

The shuttle also carries other payloads into orbit besides ordinary satellites. Many stay in the payload bay. They include large cameras and special radar equipment for photographing the Earth's surface in great detail. Another important payload is Spacelab, which is a fully equipped space laboratory. Spacelab was built by European space scientists working together under the European Space Agency (ESA).

Many satellites are launched from the shuttle from pods in the payload bay. Here a Telstar communications satellite is being sprung into orbit from the orbiter Discovery in September 1984, during mission 41-D.

On mission 51-A in November 1984, the shuttle astronauts retrieved two communications satellites that had gone into the wrong orbit. Here Dale Gardner jets over to one of the satellites and will return with it to the orbiter.

# Comsats

The most useful satellites of all are communications satellites, or comsats. They relay radio signals between the continents. The radio signals carry all kinds of information in code. This may include telephone conversations, computer data, telex messages, and television programmes.

The most powerful comsats at present are the Intelsat V series. The latest versions can handle a staggering 15,000 two-way telephone conversations at the same time, as well as two colour television channels. And the Intelsat VI series are designed to carry twice as many calls.

Most comsats are launched into a stationary orbit some 36,000 kilometres above the equator. From this high vantage point, they can communicate with countries over nearly half the world.

Comsats are full of complicated electronic equipment and are fitted with many aerials, or antennas. The aerials are tuned to receive and transmit (send out) signals at different radio frequencies, or in different wavebands. These are in the very short wave, or microwave, region.

## Satellite-Earth links

Signals are beamed up to comsats from satellite earth stations. When the signals are received, they are quite weak because of the distance they have had to travel. So electronic amplifiers on board

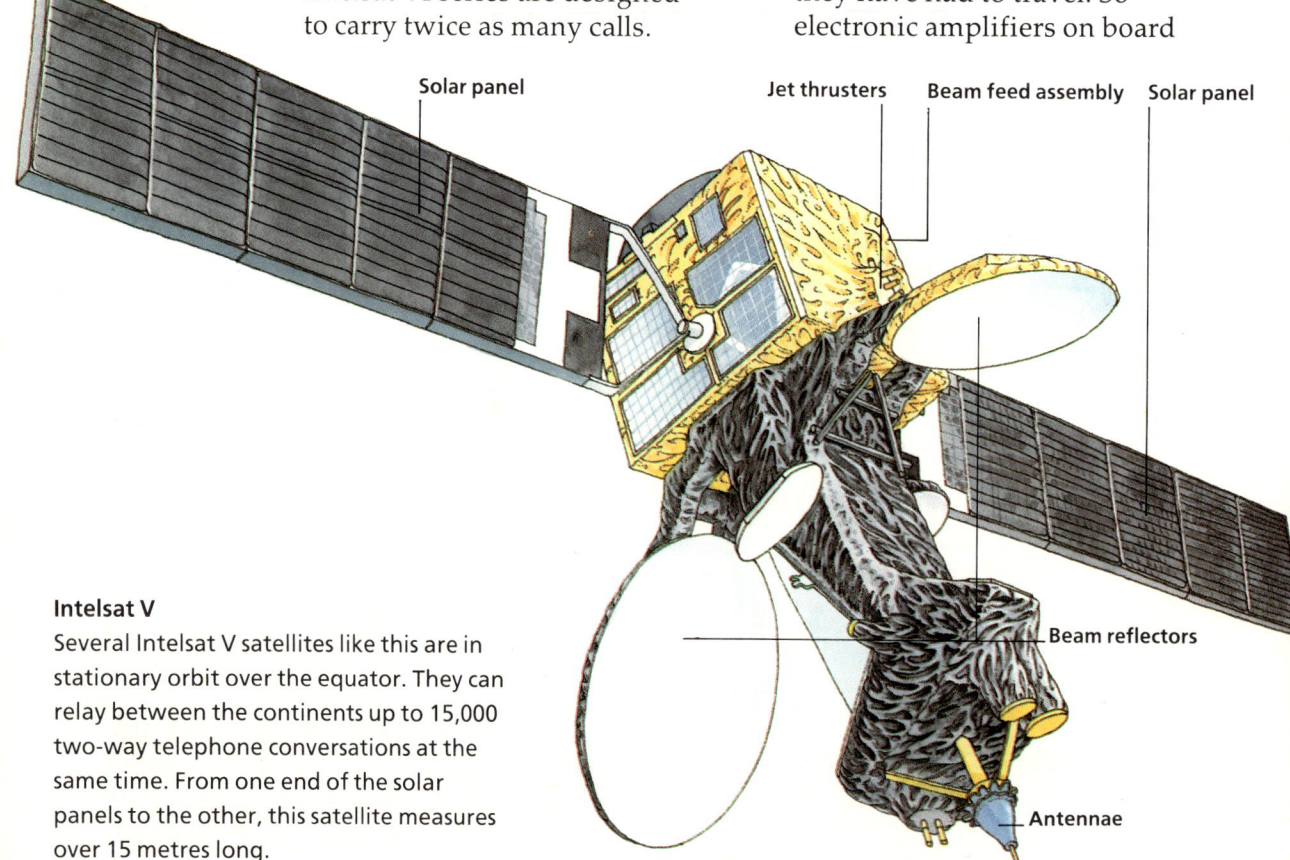

**Intelsat V**
Several Intelsat V satellites like this are in stationary orbit over the equator. They can relay between the continents up to 15,000 two-way telephone conversations at the same time. From one end of the solar panels to the other, this satellite measures over 15 metres long.

amplify, or strengthen, them. Then switching devices sort out the signals and feed them to the appropriate aerials, which beam them down to other earth stations.

To do its job properly, a comsat must always stay in the same position in relation to the Earth. This is to make sure that its aerials at all times point towards the earth stations. It must remain 'on station' over the same spot on Earth, and its attitude, or position in space must be carefully controlled. To correct any changes in position or attitude, the comsat from time to time fires little rocket thrusters. When the supply of gas for the thrusters runs out, the comsat drifts out of position and becomes useless.

After separation from its launch rocket, Intelsat V unfolds its solar panels.

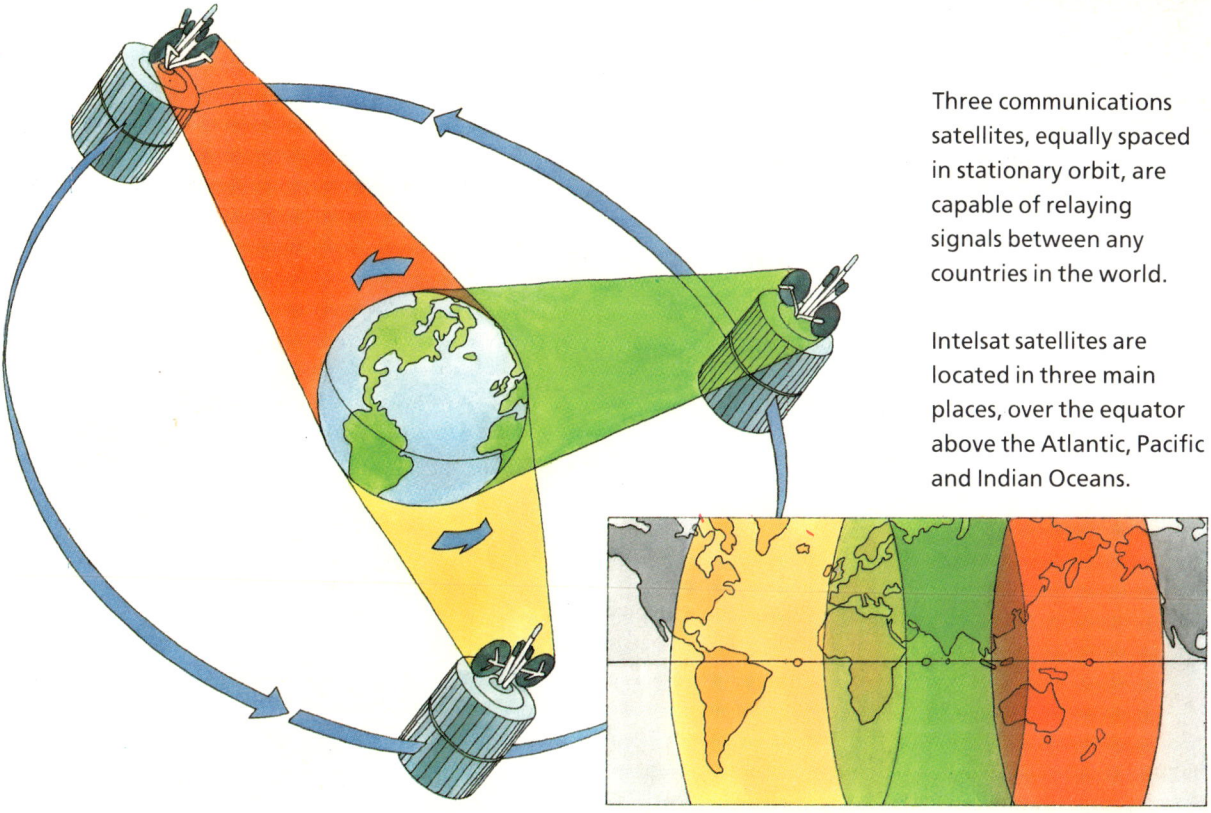

Three communications satellites, equally spaced in stationary orbit, are capable of relaying signals between any countries in the world.

Intelsat satellites are located in three main places, over the equator above the Atlantic, Pacific and Indian Oceans.

# Earth Station

Signals are sent up to and received from comsats at places called satellite earth stations. Several hundred earth stations are now in operation in more than 150 countries around the world.

The most striking features of these stations are the aerials, which are used to communicate with the satellites. The aerials are linked to a control building, which is connected by radio or cable to the normal telecommunications network (see page 22). The aerials are metal dishes that can be steered to point to any part of the sky. (Although always referred to as dishes, some aerials are very curved and rather bowl-shaped in appearance and others are flat and somewhat plate-shaped.)

## Aerials in action

When receiving, the dish gathers incoming radio signals and reflects them like a mirror to a smaller reflector mounted a little distance above it. The signals bounce off this sub-reflector into a feed horn. From there they go to the control building. When transmitting, signals are fed from the feed horn to the sub-reflector. This reflects them onto the main dish, from which they emerge as a parallel beam.

The signals that the aerial picks up from space are very weak, and have to be amplified, or strengthened. This is often carried out in the aerial itself and also later in the control building. In the aerial too, there is equipment to keep it pointing accurately at the satellite. All operations of the station are supervised and controlled by the staff from a number of instrument panels, or consoles, in the control building.

From a site in the heart of London's dockland, aerials beam signals to mainland Europe and elsewhere in the world. This new earth station is known as the London Teleport. It is operated by British Telecom. The London Teleport handles cable television transmissions and satellite business traffic.

## Station sites

One of the best-known earth stations is at Goonhilly Downs in Cornwall, England. It was one of three stations that took part in the first satellite communications tests in 1962. It now has five aerials. The biggest is Aerial 3, which has a dish 30 metres in diameter. The dish is mounted on a reinforced concrete tower 18 metres high.

Goonhilly is an excellent site for a satellite station. It is located on a plateau, which gives an all-round clear view of the sky. It is founded on solid rock hundreds of metres thick. This provides firm foundations for the heavy aerials. The site is also quite remote and is free from electrical interference, which could upset operations.

From a console in the control room of the Goonhilly earth station, an engineer adjusts the position of one of the dish aerials. Usually, however, the dish aerials steer themselves automatically to receive the strongest signals.

This satellite earth station is located at Ceduna in South Australia.

# Live via Satellite

These days, it takes only seconds to telephone someone in another country. It is easy to forget what complicated operations are involved 'behind the scenes'. When you dial or tap out the international dialling code on your phone, you get routed through to an international exchange. This switches you to a phone line that leads eventually to either an undersea telephone cable or to a satellite earth station.

In England, if your call is going via satellite, it will probably go from the international exchange via Telecom Tower in London. The tower is the hub of a nationwide network of 200 repeater stations, which relay phone calls and other information throughout the country. The calls are relayed in code in the form of microwaves, very short radio waves. From Telecom Tower, your call will pass through the network to an earth station.

At the satellite earth station, the frequency of the incoming microwave signals is altered to suit the transmitting frequency of the aerials. Then the signals are amplified and beamed up to the comsat high above.

### The global network
In England the earth stations are located at Goonhilly in Cornwall and Madley near Hereford. If the signals have to go to North America, they are routed through a comsat orbiting over the equator above the Atlantic Ocean. If they have to go to the Far East, they are routed through a comsat orbiting above the Indian Ocean.

The satellite receives the signals and beams them back down to another earth station. From there the process is reversed. The signals go via microwave relay towers and cables to an international exchange, and from there via a local exchange to the person being called.

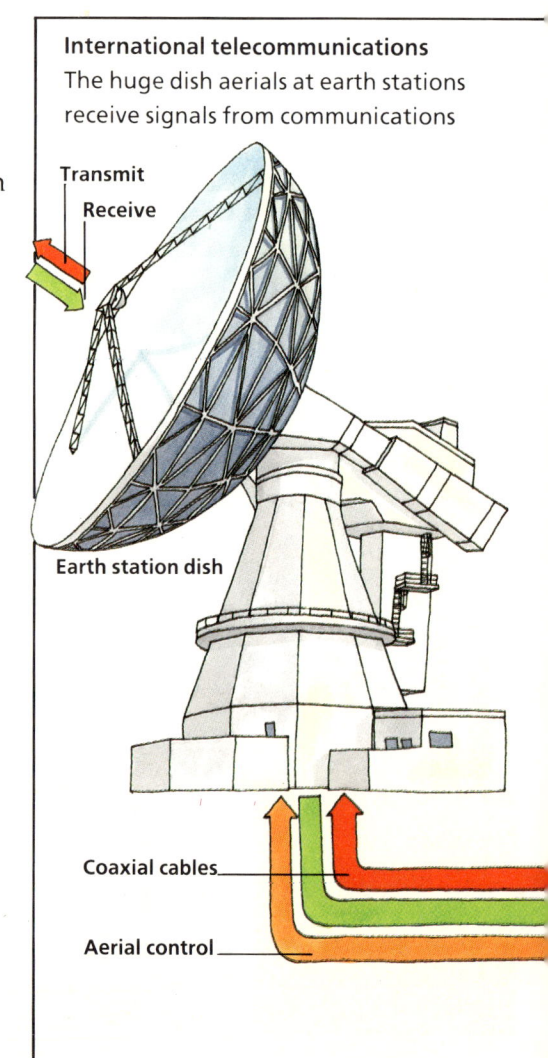

**International telecommunications**
The huge dish aerials at earth stations receive signals from communications

Transmit
Receive

Earth station dish

Coaxial cables

Aerial control

The Goonhilly and Madley earth stations are part of a network of more than 200 stations that relay telecommunications signals around the world. This network is run by Intelsat, the International Telecommunications Satellite Organization. About 110 countries belong to Intelsat, which builds and launches comsats for their use. At the moment, Intelsat operates some 20 satellites. They are all located in stationary orbits in one of three groups above each of the Atlantic, Pacific and Indian oceans.

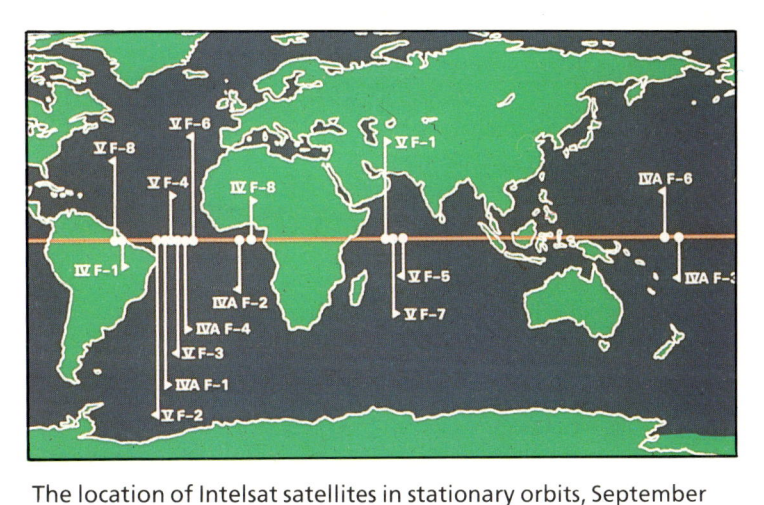

The location of Intelsat satellites in stationary orbits, September 1984. As they fail, the satellites are replaced.

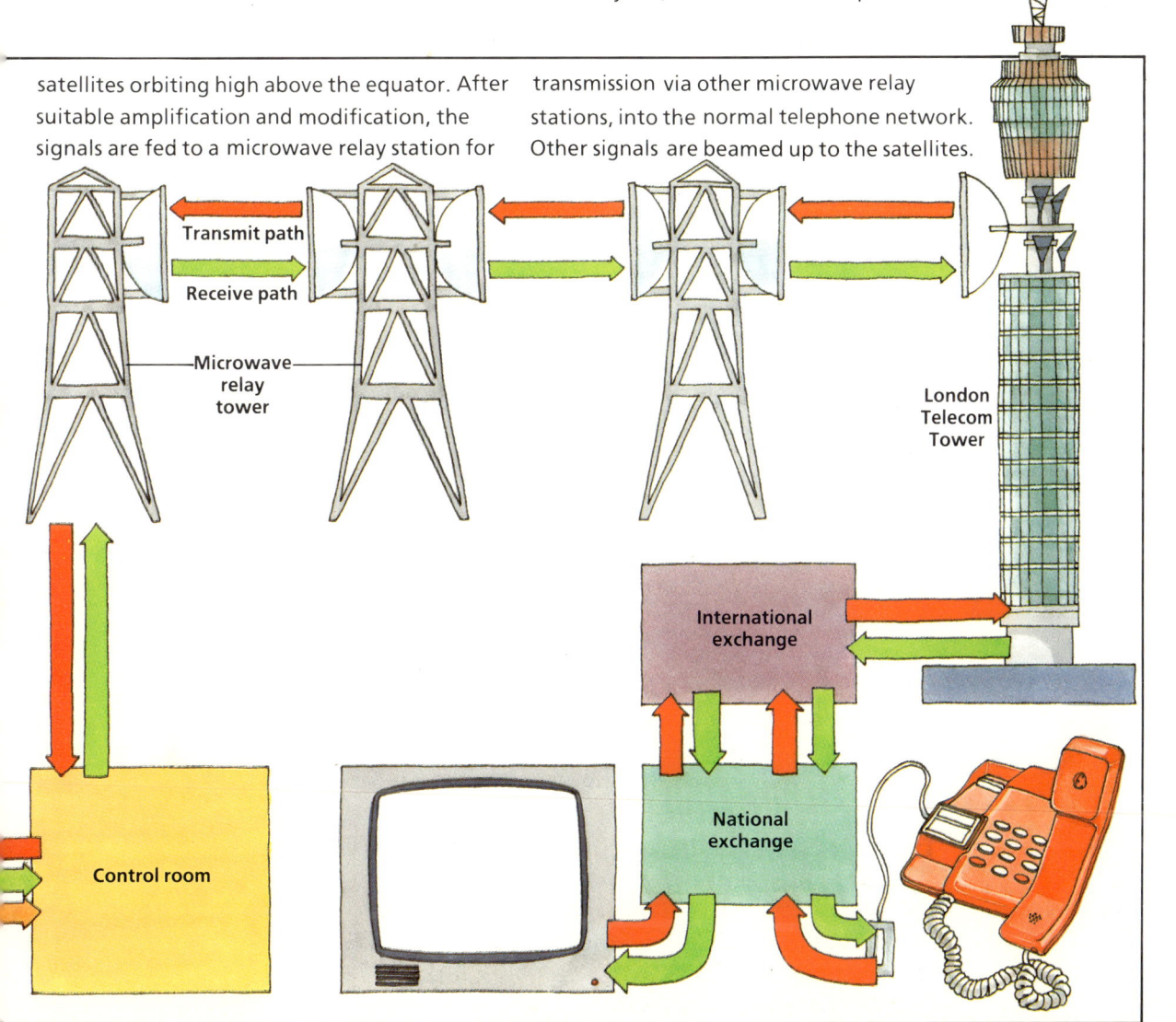

satellites orbiting high above the equator. After suitable amplification and modification, the signals are fed to a microwave relay station for transmission via other microwave relay stations, into the normal telephone network. Other signals are beamed up to the satellites.

# Special Networks

There are many other satellite communications networks in the world besides Intelsat. Many countries have their own domestic system. Canada uses Anik satellites, Indonesia uses Palapa and Russia uses Molniya. In these countries, which have a scattered population, comsats provide the most economic means of long-distance communications.

Europe also now has its own satellite communications system. This uses powerful comsats called the European Communications Satellites (ECS). They can each handle 12,000 telephone circuits and two television channels at the same time. They are in stationary orbit over West Africa. The network is operated by a consortium of European nations called Eutelsat.

Another specialized international network known as Inmarsat has been set up to cater for communications at sea. Ships virtually anywhere in the world can now tap into the international telecommunications network. They carry simple aerials and transmit/receive equipment. This puts them in contact with marine satellites such as Marecs, or with special equipment on board ordinary comsats, such as Intelsat V, which operates at the radio frequencies used by ships.

Communications from ships in the Atlantic are routed into the international telecommunication

This ship is equipped with satellite navigation equipment. The receive/transmit aerial is enclosed in the white dome.

Mending a satellite dish on a North Sea oil rig. Satellites provide a vital communications link between remote locations such as this.

system via Britain's Goonhilly earth station. The Eik earth station in Norway handles communications from the Indian Ocean, while one in Singapore covers the Pacific Ocean.

## Reaching all locations

Many business and government organizations are also using satellite communications on an increasingly wide scale, especially in the United States. The RCA Satcom series of satellites provides coverage of all the United States for television, telephone and high-speed data transmissions. They can be contacted by more than 4000 earth stations. Similar services are provided by the Galaxy and Telstar series of satellites.

In Europe, business links and data transmissions can be routed by ECS satellites using small rooftop dish aerials. The network, pioneered by British Telecom, is known as Satstream. It has proved particularly useful for maintaining contact with remote locations.

At sea, satellite communications are provided by an organization called Inmarsat. It uses Marecs and Intelsat satellites to relay signals from ships and oil rigs into the normal telephone network. The system can also handle all kinds of other signals, such as facsimile and computer data.

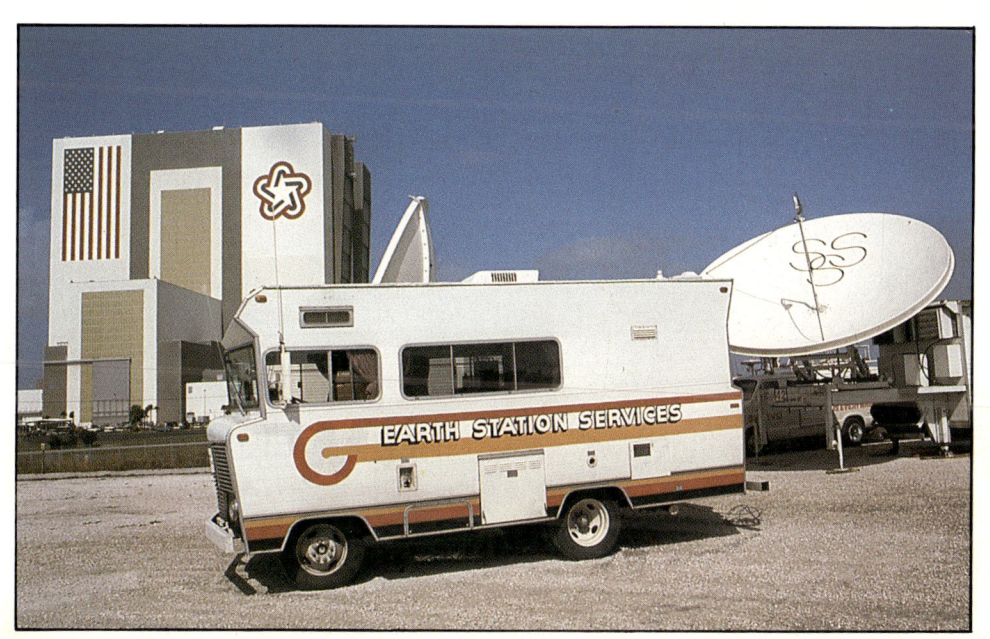

A small dish antenna set up at the Kennedy Space Center to transmit television news coverage of a shuttle launch. The news media now make extensive use of satellite communications to get the latest news from anywhere in the world.

25

# Weather Satellites

The weather satellite Meteosat being fitted into its launch rocket, Ariane. Meteosat is Europe's main weather satellite. It circles the Earth in stationary orbit above the equator in West Africa. It sends back cloud cover pictures every half-hour.

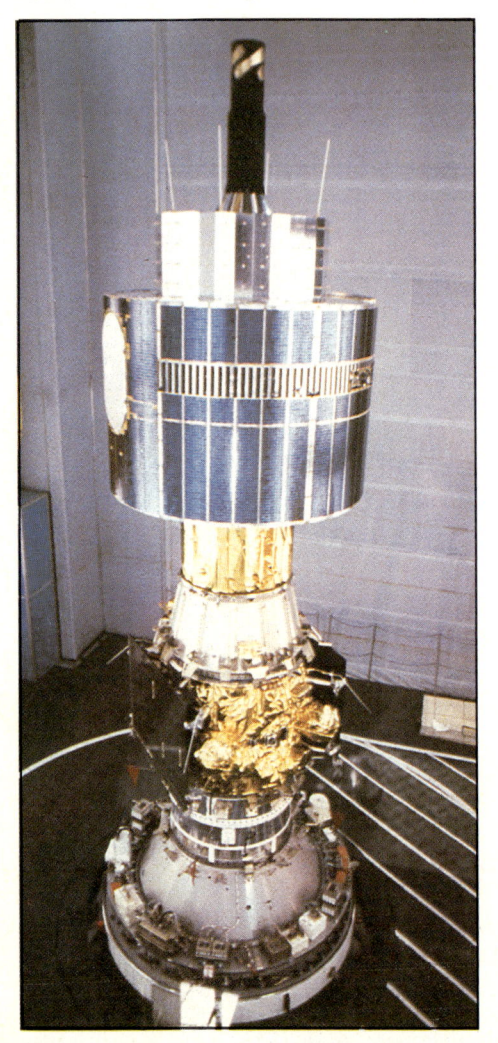

Pictures sent back to Earth by weather satellites are now a familiar part of the television weather forecast. They show the extent of cloud cover over the Earth at any time. The satellites send back these pictures regularly. This enables meteorologists, the scientists who study the weather, to follow the way the weather is changing.

Weather satellites circle the Earth in either a low or a high orbit. The Tiros and NOAA satellites, for example, orbit about 900 kilometres high in a path that takes them over the North and South Poles. They send back detailed pictures of the whole Earth but take 12 hours to do so. The GOES and Meteosat satellites circle in stationary orbit 36,000 kilometres high. They take pictures of a whole hemisphere every 30 minutes.

Weather satellites take pictures in infrared light as well as in ordinary visible light. This means they can form images at night as well as during the day. The satellites do many other things besides. They measure the temperature of the Earth's surface and at various levels in the atmosphere. They also record the amount of moisture in the air.

Some satellites also have equipment on board to relay information beamed up to them from unmanned weather platforms in remote areas of the world. These platforms record all kinds of weather data and such factors as river levels, snow depths and even earth tremors. The satellites relay the information back to meteorological centres when instructed.

### Processing the information

Meteorologists feed all the information they have received about global weather conditions into a powerful computer. This is programmed to work out how the weather patterns should develop in the future. The weathermen then use the computer predictions to make weather forecasts for their own part of the world. Because they now have so much more information at their disposal, their forecasts are much more accurate than they once were. They can issue warnings well in advance of storms, and inform motorists to beware of thick fog, black ice and other hazardous road conditions caused by the weather to come.

But don't blame the weathermen if they get their forecasts wrong! The colliding masses of air that make our weather have a nasty habit of changing strength and direction without warning.

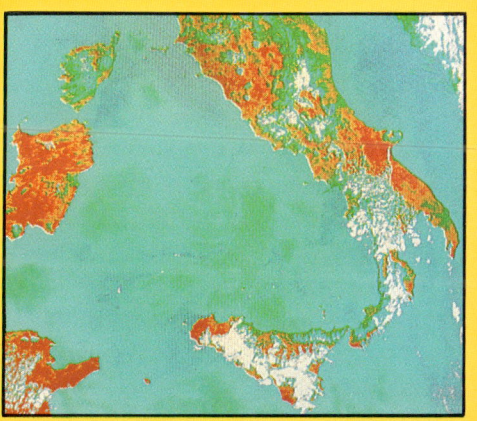

A picture of the Earth taken by Meteosat, computer processed to give natural colours.

Computer-processed weather pictures: left, temperatures around Italy; right, cloud cover over North Africa.

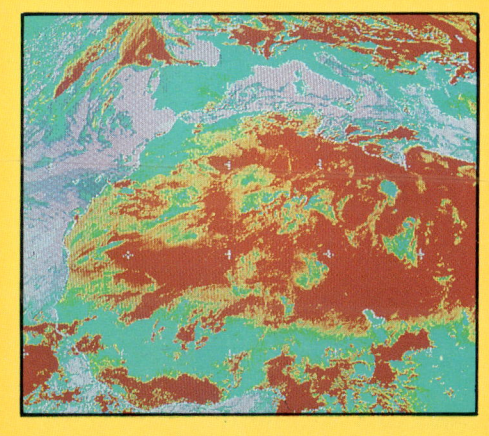

# Landsats

Landsat takes images of the Earth by a scanning device. This records features on the ground in strips 185 kilometres wide. When the strips are put together, they form a complete image.

Before the Space Age began, mapping the Earth was a long, difficult and often dangerous job. Today it is almost child's play, thanks to special kinds of satellites. These are called Earth-resources satellites because they gather information about natural resources, such as minerals, forests and crops. The best known among them are the American Landsats.

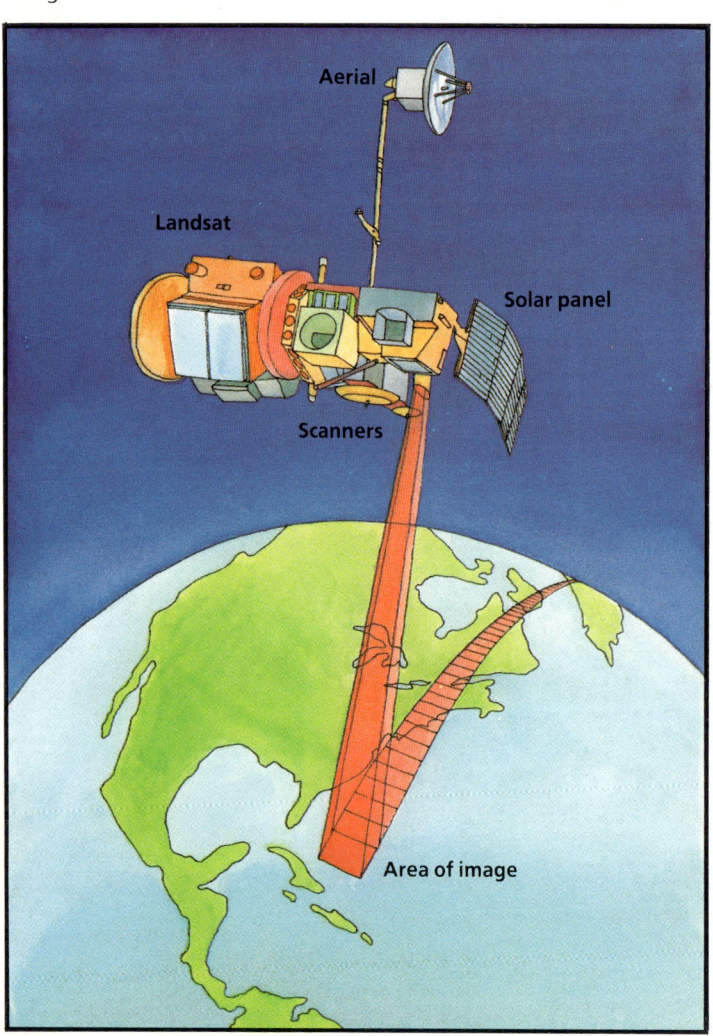

The latest one, Landsat 5, orbits the Earth at a height of 700 kilometres. It passes over the same point on the surface under the same lighting conditions every 16 days. It takes pictures, not with an ordinary photographic camera, but with scanning devices. These record pictures, or images, of the ground by scanning it, moving continuously from side to side. They record picture information as a series of lines. The information is sent back to a ground station in the form of radio signals. From these signals a recognizable image of the surface can be built up, line by line. This is similar to what happens on a television screen.

### Revealing hidden features

The scanners do not 'look' at the surface in ordinary white light. They view it in light of several different wavelengths, including invisible infrared wavelengths. Images formed at these wavelengths often show up details of the surface that are hidden in ordinary photographs.

The best way of getting information from the images is to print them in false colours. This means giving various colours to the images taken at the different wavelengths and combining them together into one picture. The colours are carefully chosen to make certain surface features stand out.

Using this method, scientists can produce images in which they can spot diseased crops in fields of healthy ones. They can see where new mineral deposits may be found. They can pinpoint sources of oil pollution. They can spot where new land development is going on.

This Landsat image of Washington DC, USA, has been processed to show the countryside in green. Roads show up white, and urban areas, pink.

A Landsat image of the Netherlands. It is printed in false colours, which show up vegetation as red.

# Star Gazers

Of all the many kinds of rays that reach the Earth from space, only visible light and radio waves can get through the atmosphere. The others have to be studied from satellites or from high-flying rockets.

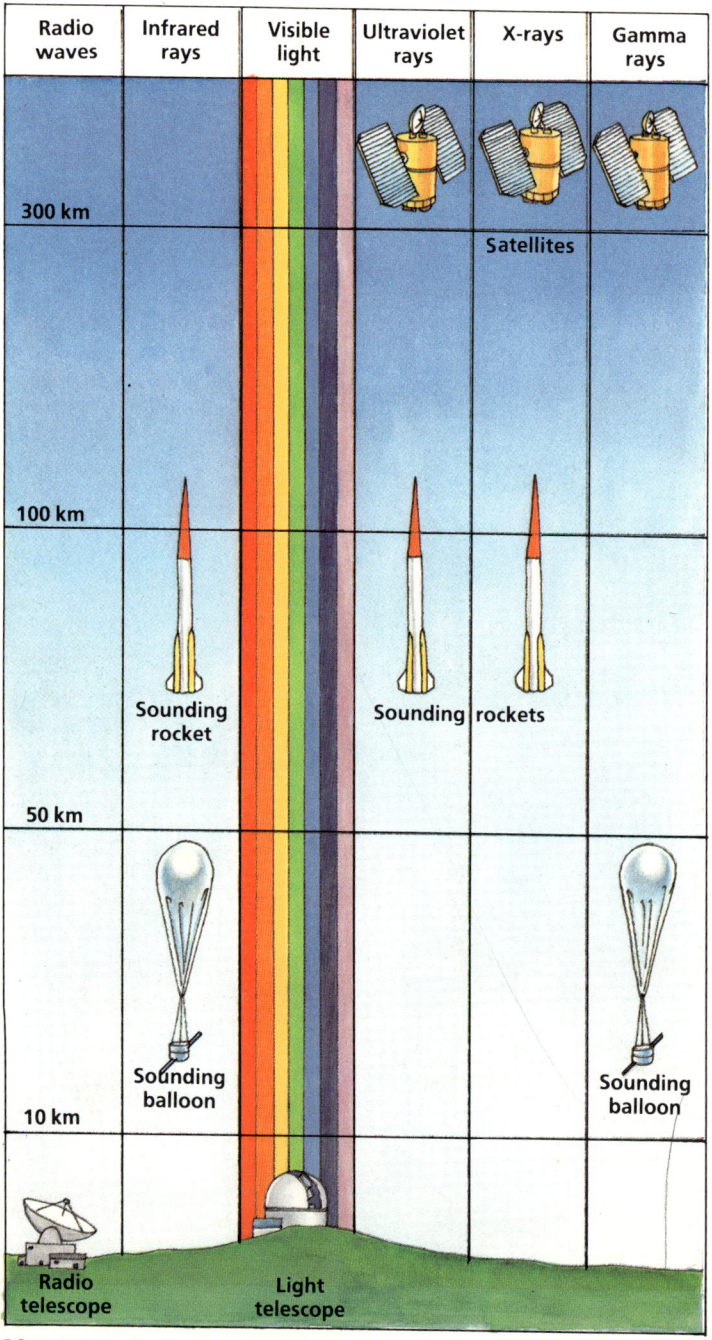

The satellites we have discussed so far 'look' down on the Earth. Astronomers, people who study the heavens, launch satellites that look the other way – into space.

These astronomy satellites have a much clearer view of the heavens than we have from Earth. This is because they orbit above the atmosphere. From Earth, the atmosphere dims and distorts the light from the stars because it contains a lot of dust and moisture.

Another reason for looking at the heavens from space is that the atmosphere blocks many of the rays the stars give out. These include X-rays and some infrared rays. They are, like visible-light rays, different kinds of electromagnetic waves. They differ in their wavelength. X-rays have a shorter wavelength than visible light, while infrared rays have a longer wavelength.

**A new view of space**

Astronomers can tell much more about a star when they can 'see' it at different wavelengths. They sometimes find that a star that looks dim in ordinary light, blazes like a beacon at other wavelengths, and vice versa. So if we could 'see' with X-ray or infrared eyes, the starry night sky would look quite different.

Using X-ray satellites like Einstein, astronomers have made many exciting new discoveries over the past few years. They have discovered heavenly bodies called bursters, which give out machine-gun like bursts of X-rays. They have found evidence of mysterious bodies called black holes, which swallow everything near them, including light.

Using infrared satellites like IRAS, astronomers have been able to see where stars are being born. They have also spied solar systems forming around other stars. There is one around Vega, one of the brightest stars in the sky.

Astronomers are now looking forward to the launch of the space telescope. This is a visible-light telescope which will be able to see five times farther in space then the biggest Earth telescope.

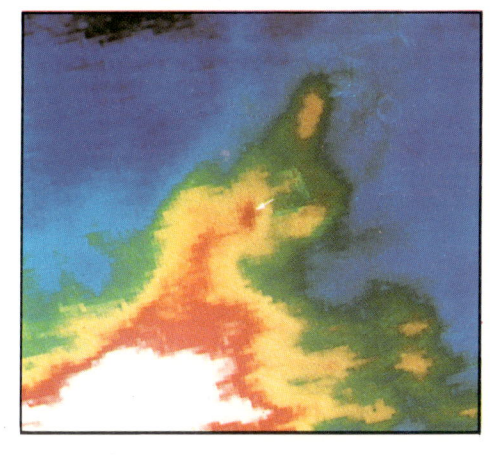

This picture shows a star being born. It was taken by an astronomy satellite called IRAS, the infrared astronomy satellite. IRAS spotted thousands of stars in the early stages of their life.

The main satellite shown here is the space telescope, scheduled for launch in 1986. It is a huge spacecraft, measuring 13 metres long and weighing 11 tonnes. It is an optical telescope, which gathers starlight with a mirror 2.4 metres in diameter. It will be able to spot stars 50 times fainter than we can see with telescopes on Earth. It will be launched by the space shuttle.

# Probing the Planets

We can learn much about the planets by studying them through telescopes. But we cannot see them very clearly because they lie so very far away. Even the closest planet, Venus, never gets closer to us than about 40 million kilometres. And most of the planets lie hundreds of millions of kilometres away.

Since the Space Age began, however, we have been able to overcome the distance barrier by sending spacecraft to explore the planets. We call these spacecraft probes. They carry cameras and a variety of instruments to detect and measure such things as magnetism, temperature, and atomic particles.

**Problems with using probes**
Naturally, it is very much more difficult to send a probe to a far-distant planet than it is to launch a

One of the giant dish aerials at the Madrid tracking station, used to pick up the faint signals coming from distant space probes. Madrid is one of the stations in NASA's Deep Space Network.

satellite into orbit. The first thing the probe must do is escape from the Earth's gravity. To do this, it must be launched away from the Earth at a speed of over 40,000 kilometres an hour, or more than 11 kilometres a second.

The probe must be very carefully aimed to reach its target. The target (the planet), of course, is moving. So the probe must be aimed to reach a point in space at the same time as the planet, maybe months, or even years ahead. Thanks to computers, this can now be done very successfully. In 1981 the space probe Voyager 2 arrived at Saturn on time after a four-year journey of nearly 2000 million kilometres!

Another major problem with space probes is communications. They are so small and travel so far that they are difficult to track, or follow. The radio signals they send out soon become very very feeble. To 'hear' them, space scientists have to use huge dish-shaped aerials. They also use these aerials to beam signals to the probes, instructing them to do things.

The radio signals themselves take hours to travel between the aerial and the probes, even though they travel at the speed of light. This means that you cannot give probes last-minute instructions when they reach the planet. They must work automatically at this time.

The path of Voyager 2 space probe through the solar system. It travelled out from the Earth, past the orbit of Mars, to Jupiter. Then it swung into an orbit that took it to Saturn. Voyager 2 then began a five-year journey to the planet Uranus, arriving early in 1986.

Voyager 2 took close-up photographs of Saturn's rings. They revealed that the rings are made up of hundreds upon hundreds of separate ringlets.

# Views from Other Worlds

Space probes have now visited all the planets that we can see with the naked eye. Going out from the Sun, they are Mercury, Venus, Mars, Jupiter and Saturn. The probes have sent back all kinds of fascinating information about the planets. But, most spectacularly, they have sent back pictures. They took the pictures with television-type cameras. And the 'pictures' came back in the form of coded radio signals. Here on Earth, the signals were decoded and converted into images by computer.

The Mariner 10 probe showed that Mercury has a rugged surface covered with craters. It looks rather like the Moon. Pioneer-Venus and Venera probes have revealed that Venus is a hellish place. On its surface the temperature is more than 450°C – hot enough to melt lead! The pressure of its atmosphere is a crushing 100 times the atmospheric pressure on Earth.

Mariner and Viking probes to Mars have shown that the planet is mainly a sandy desert. Two outstanding features of the planet's surface are a Martian 'Grand Canyon' 5000 kilometres long and an ancient volcano three times the height of Mount Everest.

**Turbulent places**
Pioneer and Voyager probes to the giant planets Jupiter and Saturn have showed them to be stormy worlds of howling hurricanes and thunderbolts. At Saturn, the Voyager probes took close-up pictures of the planet's glorious rings. These proved to be made up of little ringlets formed by lumps of rock and ice.

The Voyager probes discovered many more moons of Jupiter and Saturn, making a total of over 40 for the two planets! On Jupiter's large moon, Io, they made a surprising find, picturing a number of volcanoes erupting. It is the only other place in the solar system besides the Earth where active volcanoes are known.

The Viking 1 lander took this picture of the surface of Mars, when it landed there in 1976. This part of Mars is a flat plain. It is covered in loose soil, and rocks are scattered everywhere. The whole landscape is a rusty brown colour.

This picture of Jupiter and its four largest moons is made up of images taken at different times. The moons are Io (top left), Europa (centre), Ganymede (bottom left) and Callisto. Of these, Ganymede is the largest, with a diameter of over 5200 kilometres.

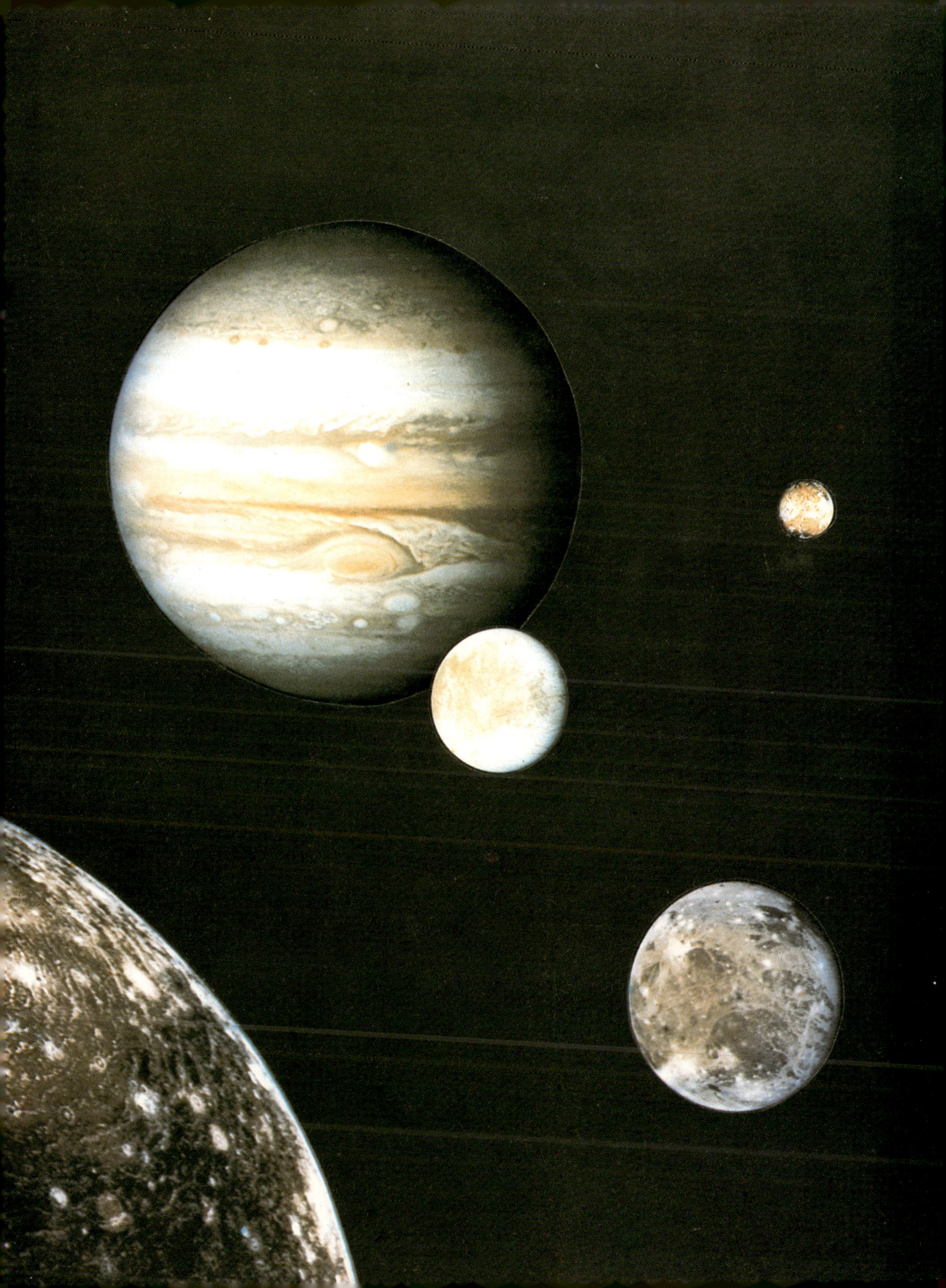

# Radio Ears

We have seen earlier (page 30) that astronomers have to send satellites into space to detect the invisible X-rays and infrared rays coming from the stars. This is because these waves cannot get through the atmosphere. But some invisible waves can get through. They are different kinds of radio waves. The people who study these waves are called radio astronomers.

Like ordinary astronomers, radio astronomers use telescopes to peer at the heavens. But their telescopes are very different from light telescopes. They are usually huge metal dishes, much like the dish aerials at satellite earth stations (see page 20). The dishes gather the faint radio waves coming from outer space and focus them on an aerial mounted above. The signals are then fed to a sensitive radio receiver, where they are amplified (strengthened) and recorded.

Two of the radio telescopes at the Parkes Radio Astronomy Observatory in New South Wales, Australia. The huge dishes pick up the faint radio signals sent out by stars and quasars.

The world's biggest dish radio telescope is at Arecibo on the Caribbean island of Puerto Rico. Its dish is more than 300 metres across (see page 38), but it cannot move. One of the biggest steerable radio telescopes is at Jodrell Bank in Cheshire. Its dish is 76 metres across. Sometimes radio telescopes in different parts of the world work together, and their results are pooled in a computer. This gives nearly the same results as would be obtained from a dish the size of the Earth!

## Looking back in time

By listening to the radio of the heavens, astronomers have made some of the most interesting astronomical discoveries of recent years. For example, they have found bodies called quasars. These are objects that look much like ordinary stars, but are millions of times farther away. They turn out to be billions upon billions of times brighter than an ordinary star. Some of these quasars lie unbelievable distances away, right at the very edge of the known universe. Their light began its journey towards us over 15,000 million years ago!

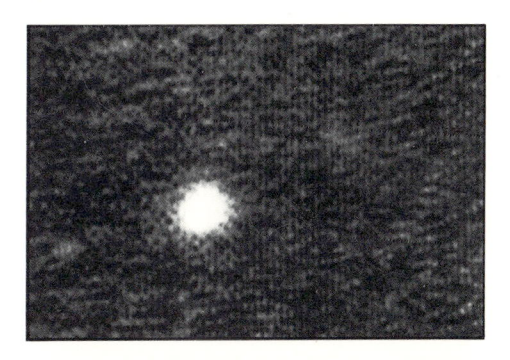

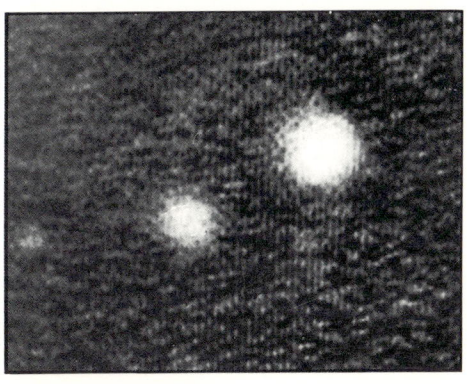

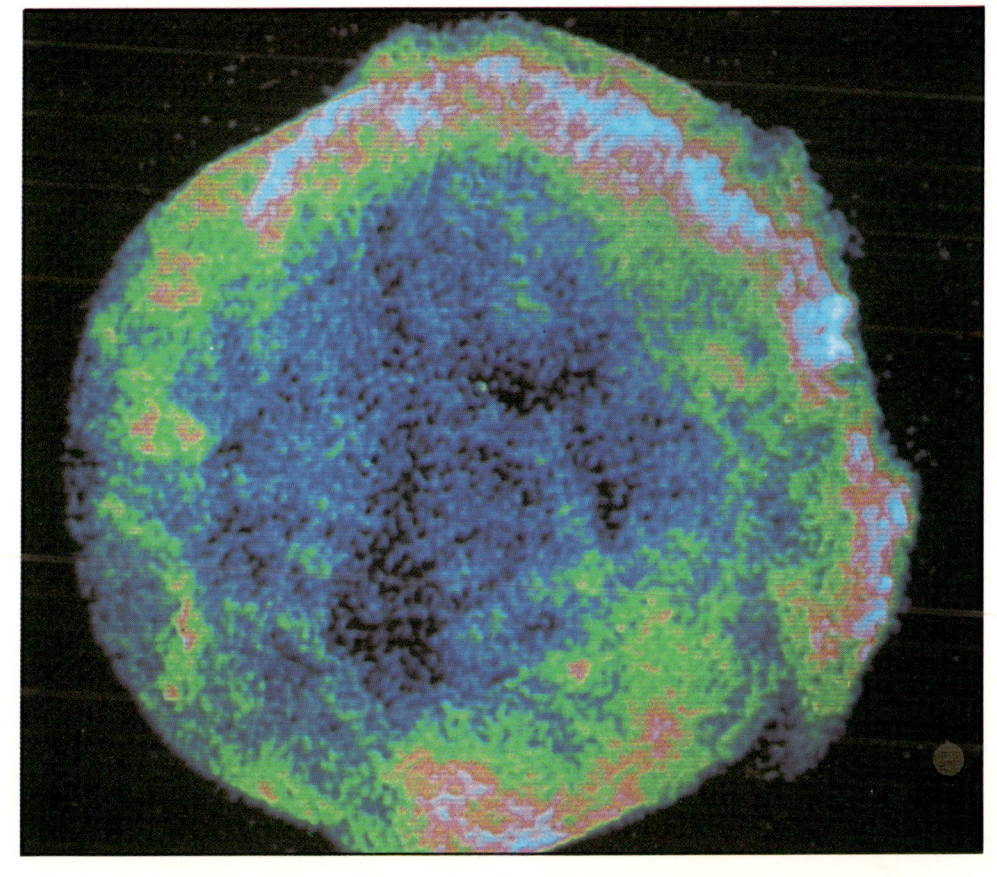

These two pictures show the 'off' (top) and 'on' phases of the pulsar in the Crab nebula. The pulsar is all that remains of a star that blew itself to pieces in the year AD 1054. Such an event is known as a supernova.

The gaseous remnants of Tycho's supernova of 1572 as visible with a radio telescope. The image has been colour enhanced by computer. The radio remnant has the form of a hollow shell.

# Alien Messages

One of the most powerful radio telescopes in the world, at Arecibo on the island of Puerto Rico, in the Caribbean. The dish reflector is 305 metres across. It is made of aluminium mesh. It scans the heavens as the Earth rotates.

In 1967 radio astronomers at Cambridge, England, picked up some curious signals coming from certain parts of the heavens. They were rapid pulses of radio waves, similar in many ways to the coded signals communications engineers send on Earth. The astronomers wondered: Could these pulses be signals from another civilization? And they called the pulsating source LGM – Little Green Men.

Alas, they soon found other sources that pulsated in the same way. These so-called pulsars are now known to be tiny and incredibly heavy stars that give off bursts of energy as they spin rapidly around.

Many people, however, now believe that there must be other intelligent life forms somewhere in the universe, probably in our own galaxy. And maybe these alien creatures are trying to make contact. If they are, they will send messages by radio, which is the speediest method of communication in space as well as on Earth. With this in mind, some radio astronomers have been listening on and off for alien communications. It is part of what is called SETI, Search for

Extraterrestrial Intelligence. As yet, no extraterrestrial messages have been received.

## Contacting other worlds

Perhaps these other beings are also listening for messages from people like us. If so, they could be in luck. Faint radio signals have been going out from Earth since the invention of radio early this century. And more powerful beams are now being sent out to communications satellites and space probes. They might by now have reached some of the nearby stars.

Some of our space probes are also now winging their way towards the stars. Many years hence, alien creatures may come across these spacecraft, which obviously have been made by an intelligent life form. They will not need to guess who we are because the probes carry the necessary information.

The Pioneer 10 and 11 probes, for example, carry plaques with the information given in the form of a coded picture. The Voyager 1 and 2 probes go one better and carry information on a disc recording. If the aliens manage to work out how to play the disc, they will be treated to a selection of natural and man-made 'Sounds of Earth'. The disc also carries in code many photographs of our planet. What a treat they have in store!

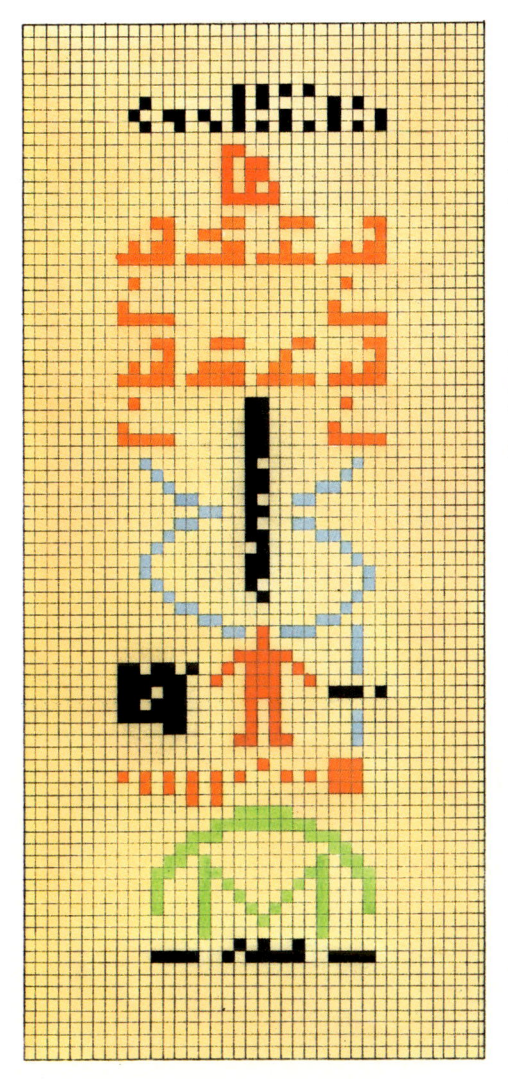

Representation of a coded message sent to nearby stars from the Arecibo radio telescope in 1974. The message gives information about life on Earth, including the shape and size of a human being and of the 'molecule of life', DNA.

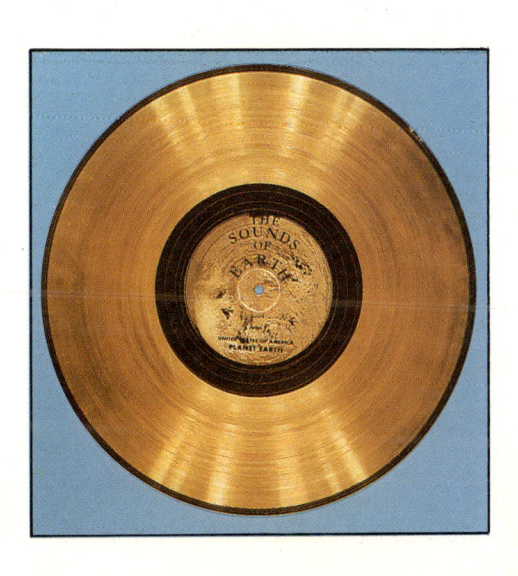

This is the kind of record carried by the space probes Voyager 1 and 2. It contains in code all kinds of information about the Earth and its people. Called Sounds of Earth, the record carries sounds ranging from babies crying to whales talking, and includes greetings to other worlds from 60 nationalities of Earth people.

# Milestones

**AD 1000s**
The Chinese invent the rocket. They use gunpowder to propel it.

**1903**
Konstantin Tsiolkovsky, a Russian schoolteacher, publishes his ideas on space flight. He suggests that rockets should be used.

**1926**
In the United States Robert H. Goddard launches the first liquid propellant rocket, which burns petrol and liquid oxygen.

**1942**
At Peenemünde in the Baltic Sea, German rocket experts carry out the first successful launching of the V-2 rocket. The V-2 is later used as a rocket bomb to bombard London.

**1945**
After World War II, V-2 rocket experts go to the United States and Russia. They begin to develop more powerful rockets that will eventually launch satellites into space.
In Britain Arthur C. Clarke puts forward the idea of communications satellites in geostationary orbit.

**1957**
Russia launches the first artificial Earth satellite, called Sputnik 1, on October 4. A month later Sputnik 2 is launched, containing the first space traveller, a dog called Laika.

**1958**
The United States launches its first satellite, Explorer 1, on January 31. It makes the first important discovery of the Space Age, sending back information about the radiation belts girdling the Earth.

**1959**
The Russian probe Lunik 3 sends back photographs of the hidden side of the Moon.

**1960**
The United States launches the first communications satellite Echo 1, a huge silvery balloon designed to reflect radio waves.

**1962**
Britain's first earth station is built at Goonhilly Downs in Cornwall.
The United States launches Telstar, the first active communications satellite (comsat).

**1965**
Early Bird becomes the world's first commercial comsat when it is launched into geostationary orbit over the Atlantic Ocean. It can relay 240 voice circuits.
Mariner 4 sends back the first pictures of another planet – Mars – over a distance of over 200 million kilometres.

**1969**
On July 20 the United States' Apollo 11 astronauts make the first live broadcast from the surface of the Moon.

**1973**
The American Pioneer 10 probe sends back the first close-up pictures of Jupiter.

**1978**
Britain's second satellite earth station is completed at Madley near Hereford.

**1979**
The first successful launch of Europe's rocket Ariane.
The Voyager 1 probe takes fascinating close-up pictures of Saturn.

**1981**
The American space shuttle makes its maiden flight on April 20. It returns to orbit again in November, becoming the first craft to make two journeys into space.

**1983**
The first powerful tracking and data relay satellite (TDRS) is launched by the shuttle.
Pioneer 10 becomes the first spacecraft to leave the solar system, still sending back signals at a distance of over 5000 million kilometres.

**1984**
The crew of the 51-A shuttle mission in November retrieve two comsats that had been put into the wrong orbit earlier in the year.

**1986**
The Voyager 2 probe sends back pictures from Uranus, over a distance of more than 2500 million kilometres.
The Intelsat VI comsat is launched, able to handle 30,000 simultaneous telephone conversations.

# Glossary

| | |
|---:|:---|
| aerial | A metal rod or dish designed to pick up radio waves. |
| antenna | Another term for aerial. |
| artificial satellite | A man-made object launched into orbit round the Earth. Usually just called 'satellite'. |
| booster | A rocket attached to the first stage of a launch vehicle that gives the vehicle additional take-off thrust. |
| communications satellite | A satellite that relays signals between different parts of the world. |
| comsat | Another term for communications satellite. |
| dish aerial | A metal bowl used to beam radio signals to, and receive them from, satellites and probes. |
| Earth resources satellite | A satellite that takes pictures of the Earth's surface from orbit. |
| earth station | A terminal in a communications network that handles the transmission and reception of signals to and from satellites. |
| ESA | Initials standing for the European Space Agency. |
| European Space Agency | The organization that controls space activities in Europe. There are 11 member countries – Belgium, Britain, Denmark, France, West Germany, Ireland, Italy, the Netherlands, Spain, Sweden and Switzerland. |
| false colour | Colour that is not true to life. Satellite pictures are sometimes printed in false colour to make certain features stand out. |
| geostationary orbit | A satellite orbit 35,900 kilometres above the Earth, in which a satellite travels once around the Earth in just 24 hours and appears 'fixed' in the sky. |
| gravity | The pull of the Earth on bodies on and above its surface. |
| Intelsat | The International Telecommunications Satellite Organization, a body set up to launch and operate communications satellites around the world. |
| Landsat | The best-known Earth resources satellite, launched by NASA. |
| launch vehicle | The rocket used to launch bodies into space. |
| Meteosat | Europe's main weather satellite. |
| microwaves | Radio waves of high frequency (very short wavelength), used for communicating in space. |
| moon | Another term for a satellite. |
| NASA | The National Aeronautics and Space Administration, the body that organizes space activities in the United States. |

| | |
|---:|---|
| orbit | The path in space of one body (say a satellite) round another (say the Earth). |
| orbiter | The main part of the space shuttle, which carries the crew and the payload. |
| oxidizer | The rocket propellant that provides the oxygen to burn the fuel. |
| payload | The cargo that a launch vehicle carries into space, usually a satellite or a probe. |
| probe | A spacecraft that travels deep into space, usually to the planets. |
| propellant | A substance burned in a rocket engine to provide hot gases for propulsion. |
| radio telescope | A telescope that collects radio waves coming from the heavens, which are given off by stars and galaxies. |
| radio waves | Waves that can be used to carry information through the air and through space. |
| remote sensing | Gathering information about something from a distance, particularly gathering information about the Earth's surface from satellites. |
| rocket | The only kind of engine that can work in space. It can work in space because it carries its own oxygen to burn its fuel, unlike ordinary engines. |
| satellite | A body that orbits round a larger body in space. The Earth has one natural satellite – the Moon – and hundreds of artificial satellites. |
| spacecraft | Any man-made body that travels in space, such as a satellite or a probe. |
| stage | One of the rocket units in a step rocket. |
| step rocket | A piggy-back arrangement of rockets used to construct a launch vehicle. Each rocket unit is called a stage. |
| telecommunications | Communications over a distance. |
| telemetry | The transmission of data and instrument readings over a distance, particularly from a spacecraft to the Earth. |
| thrust | The force that propels a rocket. |
| tracking | Following the path of a rocket or spacecraft through the air and through space, by radio or by radar. |
| weather satellite | Or meteorological satellite; a satellite that relays information about the weather, particularly pictures of cloud cover. |

# Index

Aerials 8, 9, 11, 18, 19, 20, 21, 22, 24, 25, 33, 36
Amplifiers (signal boosters) 18, 19, 20, 22, 36
Antennae *see* Aerials
Arecibo radio telescope 37, 39
Ariane rocket 12, 26
Astronauts, space shuttle 15, 16, 17
ATS-6 satellite 11

Boosters, rocket 12, 13, 15
British Telecom 20, 25

Cameras, on satellites 17, 26, 28
Cape Canaveral, Florida 13
Clarke, Arthur C. 11
Computers and computer data 18, 25, 26, 34, 37

Delta rockets 13
Discovery (space shuttle) 14, 15, 17

Earth stations 18, 19, 20, 21, 22, 24, 25, 36
Einstein satellite 30
European Communications Satellite (ECS) 24, 25
European Space Agency (ESA) 12, 17
Eutelsat 14

Facsimile transmission 25
False-colour images 28, 29

GOES (satellite) 26
Goonhilly earth station 21, 22, 23, 25
Gravity, and satellites 10, 11

Infrared pictures 26, 28, 30, 31, 36
Inmarsat 24, 25
Intelsat satellites 18, 23, 24
Interference, signal 21
IRAS (satellite) 31

Jodrell Bank telescope 37
Johnson Space Center 11

Kennedy Space Center 15, 25

Landsat (satellites) 8, 28, 29
Launch vehicles 13, 15, 16, 19, 26, 33
Little Green Men (LGM) 38

Marecs satellites 24, 25
Meteorology, satellite 8, 26
Meteosat (satellites) 26, 27
Microwave radio 18, 22, 23

NASA 11, 32
Navigation, ship 24
NOAA satellites 26
North Sea oil rigs, links with 24

Orbiter (space shuttle) 14, 15, 16
Orbits, satellite 10-11, 15, 26

Pioneer-Venus probes 34, 39
Planets, satellites to study 32-35, 39
Probes (spacecraft) 32-35, 39
Pulsars 37, 38

Quasars 37

Radar, on satellites 17
Radio signals 8, 18, 20, 24, 28, 33, 34, 38, 39
Radio telescopes 30, 36-37, 38, 39
Receivers 18, 20, 24, 36

Relay, signal 8, 19, 22, 23, 25, 26
Repeater stations 22
Rockets, for satellite launches 12-13, 15, 19, 26

Satellites
    astronomy 8, 30-38
    communications (comsats) 8, 9, 13, 17, 18-19, 21, 22, 24, 25, 39
    Earth-resource 8, 28-29
    launch 10, 12-13
    marine 24
    orbits 10-11, 15, 26
    recovery and repair 16, 17
    weather 8, 10, 26-27
    *see also* individual satellite names
Shuttle, space 14-17, 25, 31
Sounds of Earth, disc 39
Spacecraft 15, 32-35, 39
Spacelab 17
Space telescope 31
Stars, study of 8, 30-39

Telecom Tower 22
Telecommunications network 20, 22, 23, 24
Telephone
    exchange 22
    messages 18, 22, 23, 24, 25
    undersea cables 22
Teleport, London 20
Telescopes 30, 32, 36-37, 39
Television pictures 8, 18, 20, 24, 25, 26, 28, 34
Telex messages 18
Telstar satellite 17, 25
Tiros N satellite 10, 26
Transmitters 18, 20, 22, 24

Voyager spaceprobes 33, 39

Weather forecasts 8, 26-27

X-ray pictures 30, 36

43

# Acknowledgements

The editor would like to extend his grateful thanks to the many organizations and individuals who provided information and pictures for the book. He is particularly indebted to Neil Johannessen of Telecom Technology Showcase, Jane Marrow and Steve Lewington of TeleFocus at British Telecom Centre, and Joan Callieu, Kim Fitzsimmons and Sharon Cartwright at British Telecom International Publicity; to Malcolm Smythe, who created the visual presentation of his ideas; to Dee Robinson for the picture research – assisted by Francesca Wolf; and to Vivienne Canter who helped him develop the series idea when at Telecom Technology Showcase.

The designer would like to thank Graham Baylis at Dorchester Typesetting.

---

The Dataworld series of books was produced with the assistance of the Telecom Technology Showcase, British Telecom's exhibition, resource and information centre. Through a unique series of displays, videos and working models, Telecom Technology Showcase brings alive over 200 years of telecommunications history as well as offering a glimpse of the future of information technology.

Telecom Technology Showcase,
135 Queen Victoria Street,
London EC4V 4AT.
*Telephone*: 01-248-7444
*Open* Monday - Friday 10.00 - 17.00
*Admission Free*

---

PICTURE CREDITS
(T=top, B=Bottom, C=centre, L=left, R=right)
8-9 TeleFocus/British Telecom   11 NASA/Spacecharts   12 European Space Agency
13L European Space Agency   13TR NASA/Spacecharts   14 NASA/Spacecharts   16BL NASA   16-17 NASA/Spacecharts   17B NASA/Spacecharts   18 British Telecom International/NASA   20 British Telecom International
21 British Telecom International   23 British Telecom International   24T British Telecom International   24B TeleFocus/British Telecom
25 Spacecharts   26 European Space Agency
27C European Space Agency   27BL, BR Crown Copyright, Meteorological Office; *reproduced with kind permission of the Controller of Her Majesty's Stationery Office.*
29 Royal Air Force Establishment, Farnborough/Spacecharts   31T Spacecharts   31B NASA
32 Spacecharts   33C NASA   33BL NASA/Spacecharts   34 NASA   35 NASA/Spacecharts   36 Spacecharts   37T Spacecharts/Lick Observatory   37B Dr Steve Gull, Dr John Fielden/Science Photo Library
38 Arecibo Observatory   39 NASA
*Cover photo*: British Telecom International